IKHWAN

IN AMERICA

An Oral History
of the MUSLIM BROTHERHOOD
in Their Own Words

For more information about this book, visit
SecureFreedom.org

Ikhwan in America is published in the United States
by the Center for Security Policy Press,
a division of the Center for Security Policy

ISBN-13: 978-1532824937

ISBN-10: 1532824939.

The Center for Security Policy
1901 Pennsylvania Avenue, NW, Suite 201
Washington, D.C. 20006
Phone: 202-835-9077
Email: info@SecureFreedom.org
For more information, visit SecureFreedom.org

Contents

Foreword

I n 2013, the Center for Security Policy Press published *An Explanatory Memorandum on the General Strategic Goal of the Group in North America* as the first entry in its Archival Series. This collection is reproducing Muslim Brotherhood documents that have been acquired by law enforcement officials and other sources in the interest of providing insight into the nature of this shadowy organization and its methods.

The *Explanatory Memorandum* was written by a leading member of the U.S. Muslim Brotherhood network, Mohammed Akram Adlouni, in 1991 and discovered through circumstances that can only be described as providential.

In August 2004, Ismail Elbarasse was detained by Maryland Transportation Authority officers after he and his wife were observed attempting to film surreptitiously the structural supports of the Chesapeake Bay Bridge. The authorities quickly established that Elbarasse was wanted on a material witness arrest warrant in Chicago for raising funds for Hamas. The FBI obtained and executed a search warrant on the couple's home in Annandale, Virginia.

Those searches led to the discovery and confiscation of numerous documents, files, audio and video tapes on the Elbarasse property, along with an industrial-sized pallet stacked four feet high with banker-style boxes containing documents.[1] These artifacts would turn out to represent the archives of the Muslim Brotherhood in North America.

The *Explanatory Memorandum* was among the documents taken in this search and proved to be both highly revealing and explosive. It described the mission of the Muslim Brotherhood as "a kind of grand jihad in eliminating and destroying the Western Civilization from within and 'sabotaging' its miserable house by their hands [i.e., non-Muslims] and the hands of the believers...."[2]

In addition, attached to the *Explanatory Memorandum* was a list under the heading "Our Organizations and the Organizations of Our Friends." It provided the names of apparent Muslim Brotherhood front groups operating in the United States.

The memorandum would be submitted by federal prosecutors at trial as a key piece of evidence against the Holy Land Foundation, a Muslim Brotherhood-created organization whose purpose was to fund Hamas. The *Explanatory Memorandum* – when taken together with a host of other seized Brotherhood documents, surveillance records and wiretaps – helped secure the successful conviction of five co-conspirators in the largest terrorism finance trial in American history.

The damning nature of Mohammed Akhram's 1991 report prepared for the Brotherhood's leadership – and the help it provides non-experts in understanding the threat posed by the Muslim Brotherhood's "grand jihad" – has prompted a concerted effort by Islamic supremacists and their allies on the political left to try to deny its authenticity or significance. Often this has been attempted by taking the *Explanatory Memorandum* out of the context of the numerous other, supporting documents that are also in official hands, and by downplaying or simply ignoring corroborating evidence.[3]

While the release of the *Explanatory Memorandum* became a kind of Rosetta Stone for understanding the nature and character of the Muslim

Brotherhood in America, *it has never stood alone*. Its characterizations of the Brothers' mission, their plans for our country and the organizational infrastructure they have been putting into place since the early 1960s have been affirmed by numerous other documents.

It is the goal of the Center for Security Policy Archival Series to provide context and a deeper understanding of the threat posed by the Muslim

Brotherhood by publishing selections from such materials, together with analysis and explication.

It is our hope that, by providing the American public with both the original text of documents themselves along with expert evaluations of their ideological, historical and/or organizational significance, our countrymen and women and their elected representatives will be better informed about the true nature and magnitude of the threat posed to the United States by the Muslim Brotherhood.

In this, the second of our Archival Series, we feature the FBI transcript of an audiotape found during the Elbarasse search. The tape features a talk entitled "Ikhwan in America" given by the Chief Masul (Guide) of the U.S. Muslim Brotherhood's Executive Office, Zeid Noman.

This lecture by a top-level Muslim Brother before a closed Brotherhood audience serves as an authoritative oral history of the Muslim Brotherhood and their efforts in the United States *in their own words*. The talk took place in Missouri in the early 1980s, yet it foreshadows issues mentioned in the *Explanatory Memorandum* almost a decade later – including references to the Brotherhood's efforts to engage in "settlement," which the Memorandum will later come to define as a "Civilization-al-jihadist" process.

Also like the Memorandum, "Ikhwan in America" names names, including some of the most important and influential Muslim organizations in the United States. It irrefutably confirms the founding of the Muslim Students Association (MSA) and the Islamic Society of North America (ISNA) as Muslim Brotherhood entities and highlights the importance such front organizations play in the Brotherhood's stealthy and subversive civilization jihadist activities.

We hope that this newest edition will enhance the understanding of the nature and threat posed by the Muslim Brotherhood to the United States, our national security, and way of life. We encourage every American to read this volume as a further affirmation – by the Muslim Brotherhood itself – of the menace its operatives, front groups and mosques represent to our Constitution and the republic it established and the freedoms it guarantees.

Frank J. Gaffney, Jr.
President and CEO
Center for Security Policy

26 March, 2016

Preface

The document included in this volume is known as "Ikhwan in America" or, during the Holy Land Foundation trial, as Government Exhibit "Elbarasse Search-2." The document is an FBI transcript of an audiotape found in Ismail Elbarasse's home. It is the audio recording of a lecture given by Zeid Al-Noman, identified in the recording itself[4] as the General Masul of the Executive Office of the U.S. Muslim Brotherhood.

Noman himself discusses in the audiotape the importance of the Executive Office position:

> My brother, the Executive Office is the Group's Executive Leadership. The Executive Office is divided into offices. Through these offices, the affairs of the Group are run. Among them is the Organization Office..., the Organization Office which oversees the...er, over the regions and the Usras of the Group. And among them is the Education Office which oversees the preparation of cultural programs for the Ikhwans or the educational [programs] for the Ikhwans and also prepares the training programs for the Ikhwans in the different fields and various specializations among which is the Political Office which submits political analysis to the Ikhwans and also the Sisters Office which runs and promotes the activity of the Sisters Division, Among them is, of course, the Secretariat General which is the Movement's Secretary. These are the executive offices which are available now...
>
> As for the duties of the Executive Office, it executes and follows up on the works of the Group and its different bodies according to the general policy and the resolutions...., and the

resolutions issued by the Shura Council. It has to follow up and guide the activities of the general work organization and to make sure they run according to the Group's plan with what achieves its goals. It submits a periodical report to the Shura Council about its work and the activity of..., the activity of the domestic bodies and the general organizations.

Al-Noman's own position as Chief Masul of the Executive Office explains his level of access and knowledge about the inner workings of the Brotherhood in the United States and helps us to identify the significance of Mohammed Akram, the Executive Office Secretary and author of the *Explanatory Memorandum*, as a significant leader, contrary to claims by those who have attempted to dismiss the importance of the document by claiming Akram was a mere "secretary."

The FBI transcript leaves the date when the lecture was recorded unidentified, although from context clues given by Al-Noman himself we can conclude that the lecture was probably given some time around the early part of 1982, because Noman describes an executive office plan that "will be implemented beginning May '82..." suggesting it had not yet been implemented. The latest date referenced in the document is 1985, representing the last year of the most recent five-year plan, which was prepared in 1981.[5]

The timing is significant because it represents a window into the view of the U.S. Muslim Brotherhood leadership prior to the 1987 "Long Term Plan" referenced by Mohammad Akram as the basis for the *Explanatory Memorandum*. The views expressed by Al-Noman are clearly consistent with the thoughts expressed in the Memorandum, which indicates that far from being an outlying document not reflective of the Brotherhood's goals and operations, the *Explanatory Memorandum* is in line with objectives expressed at least as early as 1982, and by at least two members of the seven member Executive Office.[6] In the document, Al-Noman discusses the nature and history of the Muslim Brotherhood (using the Arabic name for the Brothers, *Ikhwan*) in the United States. He begins by discussing the early difficulties faced by the Brothers in the early '60s, as those who came to the United States, primarily as students, were more connected with the Ikhwan organizations present in their home country, and with the expectation of returning home, rather than with a united U.S.-based Brotherhood organization.

Given the role of students in the Muslim Brotherhood at this time, it's no surprise that the first Muslim Brotherhood organization founded in the U.S. was the Muslim Students' Association (MSA), founded at the University of Champlain, Illinois, in 1962.[7] Al-Noman discusses the MSA in great detail, including how early MSA conferences were also considered joint Ikhwan conferences, and membership in the MSA was a requirement for involvement with the Muslim Brotherhood in America.

Other documents discovered during the Elbarasse search confirm the Muslim Students' Association's role as a Muslim Brotherhood-controlled organization, including the *Explanatory Memorandum* [Elbarasse Search-3], and The "Historical Outlook" document [Elbarasse Search-1].

Then, Al-Noman explains how a tremendous sea change began in the U.S. Brotherhood, as a new organization and a renewed effort began to formulate a functional Muslim Brotherhood structure in the United States:

> So, the Movement then-current situation exploded during the camp of '77 and a new leadership came on board in '78 whose work was bitter as it was trying to purge the Group's body from regional restrictions and gatherings or from the organizational pockets and tied its parts together but, during this time period, it was a non-harmonious leadership and going back and forth was evident in its positions. Despite that, it managed to place the Ikhwans in front of the true picture of their reality and to shake them deeply from the inside. Therefore, the conferences of '77, '78 and '79 used to end with tears and pain but, to say the truth, were very important for what happened after that. This time period was characterized by change; a change in Ikhwans who wanted to

change the status quo and others who want to maintain the status quo. One of the things which were enacted is the attendance of the Sisters only to the Movement's conferences, only the adherent Sisters and not the wives of the Ikhwans. Also, for the first time... er, actual accountability of the leadership was enacted even though this accountability was unfair at times. In the past, leadership was seen as a group of infallible Ikhwans. Therefore, holding them accountable was rare or simple. Despite that, organizational pockets continued to constitute the biggest danger for the unity of the Group. But, this time period came to an end and the Group became more accepting of change, stability and moving forward. The elections of '79 came along and the Shura Council came in '80 and '81 and the road in front of it was paved and work began to unify the Group's ranks, codification of work and pushing the Movement's forward.[8]

Noman's invocation of the year 1977 is significant because it corresponds to the founding of the Islamic Society of North America (ISNA). Founded out of the MSA, ISNA represented the first attempt at organizing the Muslim Brotherhood outside of the student context, and directly focusing efforts and attention on activities in the United States.

This significance is confirmed in other MB-associated works of history as well. In Hisham Al Talib's "Training Guide for Islamic Workers," Al Talib, the director of the MSA's Training Department, discusses the founding of ISNA, saying:

As the MSA reached its mid-teens, it began preparing for an expanded role in the service of Islam. It called a historic meeting of a cross-section of Islamic workers in Plainfield, Indiana, in early 1397/1977. This meeting set up a task force to recommend a new organizational structure to respond to the increasing challenges and responsibilities emerging in the growing North American Muslim communities. The task force concluded a new environment would be best served by establishing a broader umbrella organization called the Islamic Society of North America. This was accomplished during Rabi'al Awwal 1403/ January 1983.[9]

Al Talib has a number of connections to known Muslim Brotherhood groups, including the International Institute of Islamic Thought (IIIT) and the suspected Al Qaeda/Hamas finance group Al Taqwa Bank.[10]

Elbarasse Search-1, "Historical Outlook" also confirms the central importance played by ISNA, defining it as the "nucleus of the Islamic Movement."[11]

Another important event taking place in 1977 were major changes made by the Islamic Circle of North America (ICNA), the front organization for Jamaat-e-Islami (JeI) in the United States. Beginning in 1977 "ICNA established forums for Dawah work at the local, regional and national level." Also in 1977, Shamim A. Siddiqui, a JeI member from Pakistan before immigrating to the United States, founded "The Forum for Islamic Work." Siddiqui would go on to be the chairman of ICNA's Dawah committee and the author of "Methodology of Dawah," a seminal piece of Islamist literature regarding operations in North America, and which provides details for a phased set of "milestones" by which JeI could implement its Dawah in North America.[12]

The creation of ISNA and ICNA's reorganization would set the stage for the eventual merger of the "Islamic Circle" with the Muslim Brotherhood, as mentioned in Akram's *Explanatory Memorandum*.

Having discussed how the Muslim Brothers were able to coalesce and focus themselves on activities in North America, Al-Noman discusses what those plans were:

> The main goals which were approved by the executive office were five...., which were put together by the executive office and which were then approved by the Shura Council were,

first of all: Strengthening the internal structure; second, administrative discipline; third, recruitment and settlement of the Dawa'a; four, energizing the organizations' work; five, energizing political work fronts. Also, it adopted eight of the secondary goals on top of which were: finance and investment; second, foreign relations; third, reviving women's activity; four, political awareness to members of the Group; five, securing the Group; six, special activity; seven, media; eight, taking advantage of human potentials.

Most notable among these are the reference to "recruitment and settlement of the Daw'a."

Dawa, meaning preaching or proselytizing, is an Islamic religious obligation to spread the word of Islam and invite non-believers into it. It also bears importance in the performance of Jihad, since Dawa can be viewed as obligatory before Jihad may commence.[13] The concept of Dawa bears substantial importance to the Muslim Brotherhood, following the methodology imparted by major Ikhwan ideologue Sayyid Qutb, who noted:

> This movement uses the methods of preaching and persuasion for reforming ideas and beliefs, and it uses physical power and Jihad for abolishing the organizations and authorities of the Jahili system which prevents people from reforming their ideas and beliefs, but forces them to obey their erroneous ways and make them serve human lords instead of the Almighty Lord.[14]

Al-Noman makes clear he is referring to the Muslim Brotherhood's view of Dawa as a means to establish itself and its authority, not a kind of general proselytizing. He explains:

> By "settlement of the Dawa'a", the Muslim Brotherhood Dawa'a is meant. It is not meant to spread Islam as spread of Islam is a general thing and it is indeed a goal for each Muslim in general terms.

For readers who have examined in detail the *Explanatory Memorandum* document, the discussion of "settlement" will be familiar as a "Civilization-jihadist" process.

As Al-Noman continues his discussion of the settlement of Dawa, he discusses how the Brothers from the MSAs began to acquire off-campus properties for use as "Islamic Centers" in order to reach out the broader Muslim community, and conduct dawa:

> This was also another healthy move for settling the Dawa'a as the presence of an Islamic center means the presence of residents, means the existence of contacts between students and the residents, means recruitment of the and winning them to the ranks of the Dawa'a, means forming permanent foundations in these cities. Then, what we have now or what we feel now is that there a bigger and bigger acceptance than the Ikhwans' base for this change and we ask God the Almighty to help us so that we can finish this mission which is the settlement of Dawa'a and that, by that, we would have permanent foundations in America which can benefit Islamic work generally speaking and may God reward you all good.

Again, this same view appears in the Memorandum, as Akram describes the centrality of the Islamic Centers by saying:

> In brief we say: we would like for the Islamic center to become "The House of Dawa'" and "the general center" in deeds first before name. As much as we own and direct these centers at the continent level, we can say we are marching successfully towards the settlement of Dawa' in this country.[15]

Additional goals, listed among secondary goals but still worthy of mention, include Al-Noman's reference to "securing the Group" and "special activity." While these terms may appear vague, their meaning is addressed within the content of the tape itself, as Noman answers a question from one of the unidentified brothers in the audience:

> **Um (Unidentified Male):** By "Securing the Group", do you mean military securing? And, if it is that, would you explain to us a little bit the means to achieve it.

> **Ze:** No. Military work is listed under "Special work". "Special work" means military work. "Securing the Group" is the Groups' security, the Group's security against outside dangers. For instance, to monitor the suspicious movements on the...., which exist on the American front such as Zionism, Masonry....etc. Monitoring the suspicious movements or the sides, the government bodies such as the *CIA, FBl...etc*, so that we find out if they are monitoring us, are we not being monitored, how can we get rid of them. That's what is meant by "Securing the Group".

This is an interesting and revealing statement by Al Noman because it indicates that the Muslim Brotherhood, even in the United States in 1982, had not abandoned its devotion to potentially violent means (military work) nor had it given up training its members for potential violent conflict against its opponents. This is contrary to much of the analysis of the Obama Administration, which has described the Brotherhood has possessing a "decades-long commitment to nonviolence."[16]

The term "special activity" or "special work" is reminiscent of the original Muslim Brotherhood terrorist wing, created by the founder Hassan Al-Banna and known within the Brotherhood as the "special section" or to outsiders as the "secret apparatus." Richard P. Mitchell, author of "The Society of the Muslim Brothers," describes the Secret Apparatus thusly:

> Inspired in the first instance as an idea by the concept of jihad, formalized into an organization under the pressures of nationalist agitation, the secret apparatus was almost imme-

diately rationalized as an instrument for the defence of Islam and the Society. In 1943 it began to play the part of the defender of the movement against the police and the governments of Egypt."[17]

In addition to carrying out terror attacks, the Secret Apparatus helped prepare Muslim Brotherhood's "battalions" for Jihad in the Palestine Mandate beginning in 1947.[18] While Noman doesn't reference the battalions in the audiotape, they are mentioned in the *Explanatory Memorandum*, where Akram describes the importance of using Islamic Centers to "Supply our Battalions".[19]

Noman confirms that the Brotherhood in the United States was also preparing for violence in response to a question raised on the tape:

> If the asking brother is from Jordan, for instance, he would know that it is not possible to have military training in Jordan, for instance, while here in America, there is weapons training in many of the Ikhwans' camps.

Noman goes on to describe a situation in Oklahoma, where he states that weapons training had become impossible after local camping areas began requesting identification in order to rent campgrounds with shooting facilities.

As with Noman's concerns regarding showing identification, his statements regarding the necessity of "securing the group" from surveillance by the FBI and CIA are also reflective of the nature of the Muslim Brotherhood's behavior. Noman's statement takes place at least five years prior to the Muslim Brotherhood's founding of Hamas, and 15 years prior to Hamas' designation as a terrorist organization by the United States, yet clearly the Brotherhood was aware that they were engaged in seditious and potentially criminal activities that would likely raise the attentions of law enforcement and intelligence.

We have reason to believe that the Muslim Brotherhood was in fact taking serious steps to conduct military training and to engage in intelligence and counterintelligence activities, thanks to the 1995 search by federal law enforcement officials of the home of convicted (and since deported) Muslim Brotherhood member and Palestinian Islamic Jihad organizer Sami al-Arian.[20] Additionally, Al-Arian was himself a co-founder of ISNA.[21]

The search uncovered a document that was described by law enforcement as the charter for a "hostile intelligence organization."[22] The "Charter" was dated June 1981, and while we can not be sure that Al-Noman was aware of it, he may have been as the Charter calls for the new intelligence organ to answer to the General Chief (Masul), executive bureau (presumably meaning the same thing as the Executive Office) and the Shura Council, possibly referring to positions which Noman in fact held.[23]

While obviously concerning, the Brotherhood's willingness to train its members in violence and prepare for "military work" is a secondary goal. One of the primary goals, the energizing of "political work fronts," provides a wider window into the way the Brotherhood operates in the United States.

Noman explains in response to a question that the use of fronts is critical to the Brotherhood's operations in the United States. According to the Chief Masul, the Muslim Brotherhood front organizations represent more than the personal energies of their participants without wider co-ordination. Rather, Noman indicates that each front that has been created was done so deliberately and with great consideration.

Noman explains:

> By God, fronts are one method....., one method for grouping
> and are one method to communicate the Ikhwan's thought.
> They are one method to communicate the Ikhwan's point of

view. A front is not formed until after a study and after an exhaustive study. I mean, the last front formed by the Group is the Islamic Association for Palestine. So, Ikhwans, this did not come out over night or it was not like the Ikhwans who are in charge went to sleep, dreamed about it and met the next day and decided to do it. Not at all, by God. This went through lengthy meetings and took long discussions. Many specialized auxiliary committees were formed which were examining this work, they were examining this work from different angles, from the angle of the benefit of such work, from the angle of, for instance, the human resources we have, from an angle of how this front would benefit us in com- municating the brothers' point of view.

Note the reference to the Islamic Association for Palestine (IAP), one of the organizations of the Palestine Committee of the Muslim Brother- hood. IAP is described in the U.S. Government's Trial Brief in the Holy Land Foundation Trial as a "media and propaganda organization."[24] IAP received almost $757,864 from Hamas leader Mousa Abu Marzook from 1985-1992.[25] Ismail Elbarasse, in whose home the documents were found, was also a member of the Islamic Association of Palestine.[26] IAP members also included Omar Ahmad and Nihad Awad, who would go on to found the Council on American Islamic Relations (CAIR), which was itself listed as an organization of the Palestine Committee.[27]

Additionally, Noman explains how through the use of fronts the Broth- erhood is able to have a larger impact than their membership would otherwise dictate:

But, an active and a smart brother can benefit from the ef- forts of the Islamists who are around him, for instance. He can distribute some of these burdens in a way which does not let planning get out of the hands of the Group in the re- gion. He can benefit from the resources around him because we, Ikhwans, cannot work with our resources alone and our number is limited. So, let every brother check the percentage of the Ikhwans against the number of existing Muslims and not the entire Muslims. But, let's say, the adherent Muslims who attend the Friday prayers, for instance. If you check the percentage, you won't find the Ikhwans percentage in people more than 1% which is a tiny percentage, of course. It is possible, of course, that you think that this 1% can not carry the entire work burden. But, if you manage to direct the resources which are available to it and when you can benefit from it, this burden will then become less.

The use of fronts helps to underline how Muslim Brothers, even while they may personally represent a minority of the Muslim population in the United States, are able to exercise oversized influence over area mosques, Islamic Centers, and national and regional Muslim organizations under their control.

Taken in its totality, the Al-Noman audiotape "Ikhwan in America" is an important piece of historical evidence. It helps to show how the the Muslim Brotherhood established itself in the United States and had not, as late as 1982, moved away from its original goal of engaging in violent jihad, overthrowing non-Islamic governments, and establishing itself as the dominant Islamic power. "Ikhwan in America" confirms and provides context for much of what we know about the Muslim Brotherhood's ongoing plan for America, as it is described in the *Explanatory Memorandum.*

"Ikhwan in America" is a must read for any student of the depth and nature of Brotherhood activity in the United States. We present it in its entirety, without edits, and as close as possible to the format in which it was submitted at trial.

Date/Time Recorded:

Tape Number/CD #:   T13-T18 1 "Ikhwan in America. Zeid"

Participants:

Ze = Zeid al-Noman
Um = Unidentified Male

Abbreviations:

Italics	Spoken in Foreign Languages
IA	Inaudible
UI	Unintelligible
PH	Phonetic
[ ]	Background Conversation / Noise/Translator's comments
SC	Simultaneous conversation

Side A:

Um: I resort to God from the pelted Devil. In the name of God, the Beneficent, the Merciful. Thanks be to God and prayers and peace be upon God's messenger, his family and his companions. Brothers, God's peace, mercy and blessings to you. Er...., these special meetings in which the Ikhwans meet in organizational meetings there is a good opportunity to meet the Ikhwans, for their cooperation and an opportunity to exchange advice with each other and...[UI]. They are also an opportunity for the Muslim Ikhwans to meet in this Dawa'a and they are also a good opportunity for the brothers the Masuls of this Dawa'a to meet their brothers in their locations and in their activities. And..., and today in our lecture, we meet with a Masul brother so that the Ikhwans can express what is in their hearts and so that you can benefit from the directions of the Masul brother and that's it.

We just would like to remind you that..., of course, the title of the lecture is "The Ikhwans in America" but the questions which will follow the lecture will not be limited to the subject presented by the brother but will include any general....., any questions..., any question a brother wants to pose or present around the Dawa'a in America. We now meet brother Zeid al-Noman, Masul of the Executive Office, may God reward him all good.

Ze: Thanks be to God, Lord of the Two Worlds. Prayers and peace be upon the master of the messengers, Mohamed Bin Abdullah and all of his family and companions. My brothers, God's willing, I will speak about...er, our history. I will begin with a historical outlook....er, about the history of the Muslim Brotherhood Movement in north America. After that, I will go ahead and speak about the nature the Movement in north America and what are the difficulties which face work over here. I will then conclude the lecture, God's willing, ... [coughing] ... I will then conclude the lecture, God's willing, by talking about priorities of work in north America as compiled by the Executive Office. The Movement was founded...., the Movement was founded here with the founding of the general Islamic activism or it might have preceded it by a little bit. At first, it was a gathering or a grouping for Islam activists without an organizational affiliation with the Movement. So, the first generation of the Muslim Ikhwans in north America composed of a team which included he who was an Ikhwan in his country or he who was a member of The Worshipers of the Merciful Group or he who doesn't have a direction but who is active in Islamic activism. This was the first point or group which gave or planted the Muslim Brotherhood seed in America.

After that, the Movement went through different organizational formats. One of the first organizational formats tried here were the regional gatherings as each movement had...., had its gathering with a leadership and the collection of these leadership formed the Group's leadership or what is called the Coordination Council. They were meeting and the resolutions of that Council were non-binding for its members. Of course, there were some countries...., there were some countries which did not have a large gathering in north America, we can call them .... [UI] countries, individuals of this country would associate with the nearest movement to them. So, for instance, an Iraqi might have joined Jordan's Ikhwans and, for instance, a Libyan might associate with Egypt's Ikhwans and so forth.

Following this stage, a new organizational format started to evolve which is the unified Movement. These...., these groups of Ikhwans started to gather under one leadership. During this stage, the name of this gathering was not important but the affiliation with the Ikhwan's name was an affiliation due to the size of thought of this Movement and...er, or books and writings of this Movement which were available in the field. This was the reason for which the name "The Muslim Brotherhood" was adopted as a basis for this work. I mean, to the point that, at some point, there was an attempt to change the name of the Muslim Brotherhood Movement to The Islamic Movement and making it affiliated with a dissenting group in Iraq called the Islamic Movement. All of that, Ikhwans, was at the beginning of work when the Ikhwans who came to America, may God reward them all good, were seeking methods for activism. This was probably in mid 60's...er, or even .... , I mean, mid 60's, long time ago. As for recruitment in the ranks of this Movement, its main condition was that a brother...., was that a brother must be active in the general activism in the MSA, a person who attends its general conferences or participating in its executive committees, whether local or central, and this was the Movement's condition in the 60's.

We can then sum up the condition of the Movement in the 60's by saying that commitment to the Movement was a sentimental commitment, a grouping one, and general activism was the basis for that commitment. Also, in the beginning there were regional gatherings which turned into a unified Movement without an intellectual or organizational scale. And we said that recruitment used to take place in the following format: attending the MSA conferences and choosing active Arab elements and approaching them to join the Ikhwans. This was followed by visits to the local branches and, consequently, choosing active elements over there and approaching them to join the Ikhwans. As for the Ikhwan who came from their countries, they most probably joined the Movement specially if there were large numbers of the Ikhwan Movement who preceded them to America. Then, joining the Movement would be automatic; he would notify that he has arrived and, after that, he would join in the nearest opportunity.

Most of the Usras then were individual Usras. I mean, sometimes an Usra would be made up of three people and the distance between two of them is maybe 100 or 150 miles, They would meet once a month or once every six weeks, After that period, in the beginning of the 70's a new era started. We can call it the stage of codification. The people started to..., they put together the first bylaws of theirs and they started after that to.... And, in doing this thing, there started to be an emphasis on the Ikhwan's formula for this Movement. Prior to this stage, young elements came to America, specially Gulf elements or Saudi elements which joined the ranks of the Movement regularly. This was the first true tremor for the Ikhwan's activism here in America as these brothers started to demand clearer Ikhwan formulas, clearer commitment and means or ones with a specific and not a general nature and that there are conditions to accept one into the ranks of this Dawa'a and to made work secret....etc.

This characteristic....er, this current started to come to surface or this current started to be distinguished in Islamic activism during the ranks of the Movement to the point that The Shura Council appointed to it a brother who represents this direction even though he is not elected to that Council. If we examine the Group's conferences in this..., in this time period, we would find that they were characterized with the following: First of all, in the past the Ikhwans' conferences used to be held in the same time as the MSA 's conferences, at the same time. They would either precede it with one day or come a day after them. After that they became separate from the MSA 's conferences and they lasted an entire week. Also, the leadership would be elected during these conferences. We notice that there used to be a family characteristic to these conferences, that a brother would attend and his wife and children even if his wife is not a Sister. Also, attending this..., this meeting were some of those working in the Islamic field and, particularly, the brothers in the Ilalaqa, the Beloved Halaqa which is the Pakistani brothers' Movement or the brothers who were members of the Islamic Group in Pakistan and came to America. This period continued until..., until approximately the year '75 and after that the era of dedication for the general activism began. During this time period, leaders of the Group were dedicated to the general activism organizations which were in the formation phase which took a lot of their time and all of that was at the expense of the Movement and the special domestic activism.

During this time period, there was a big desire to come to America to study and large delegations of youth come to the country, most of whom were committed to the Dawa'a in his native country. During the..., during the same time, the Ikhwans' foreign connections became strong and that was due to the fundraising campaigns which were launched by the Ikhwans..., which made it possible for the Ikhwans in the leadership to meet leadership from the Orient. Therefore, membership here of the brothers who were members in their countries was easier, more easier. Those people come to the Movement and found some organizational practices such as means and priorities which were different from the ones they were accustomed to in their countries. So, they started to inquire, "Where is the strictness in the conditions? And where are these conditions? Where is the secrecy, where is organizational connection and where are the educational programs? What are goals of the Group here? What are goals of..., the goals of these programs?"

All of these questions were resurfacing on the field anew. Therefore, regional organizational pockets started to form during this time period. Also, rumors and suspicions started to circulate among the ranks of the Group regarding individuals in the leadership. So, the Movement then-current situation exploded during the camp of '77 and a new leadership came on board in '78 whose work was bitter as it was trying to purge the Group's body from regional restrictions and gatherings or from the organizational pockets and tied its parts together but, during this time period, it was a non-harmonious leadership and going back and forth was evident in its positions. Despite that, it managed to place the Ikhwans in front of the true picture of their reality and to shake them deeply from the inside. Therefore, the conferences of '77, '78 and '79 used to end with tears and pain but, to say the truth, were very important for what happened after that.

This time period was characterized by change; a change in Ikhwans who wanted to change the status quo and others who want to maintain the status quo. One of the things which were enacted is the attendance of the Sisters only to the Movement's conferences, only the adherent Sisters and not the wives of the Ikhwans. Also, for the first time....er, actual accountability of the leadership was enacted even though this accountability was unfair at times. In the past, leadership was seen as a group of infallible Ikhwans. Therefore, holding them accountable was rare or simple. Despite that, organizational pockets continued to constitute the biggest danger for the unity of the Group. But, this time period came to an end and the Group became more accepting of change, stability and moving forward. The elections of '79 came along and the Shura Council came in '80 and '81 and the road in front of it was paved and work began to unify the Group's ranks, codification of work and pushing the Movement's forward. For the first time then, we had a General Masul who was dedicated to the Group's affairs alone and also the Shura Council started to play its true role which is planning and monitoring the executive leadership.

The executive leadership was carrying its tasks through a Shura atmosphere and continuous contacts. Its meetings were held consistently on monthly basis. The mid-level leadership which was represented by the Masuls of the regions and the regions' councils play their natural role as well through applying the principle of decentralization. Work started to be clearer and more programed. The current Shura Council came on board to finish what its brother started on the span of past seven years to lead this Group to new horizons, God's willing, keeping its eyes on huge goals among which is the settlement of this Group and minding some of the regional experiences and the turns of the Muslim Brotherhood Movement in north America. This is a quick narration for the history of the Muslim Brotherhood in north America and, as you notice, it is not old history, I mean, the Movement started here in the 60's and we are now in the 80's. That means that the Movement's age is between 15 and 20 years only. Despite of that, the result of the experience...., the experience Movement went through, is large and it made it possible to short-cut many years as a result of the fusion of different experiences which came from different backgrounds. After that, we examine what..., what is the nature of this Movement after it gained it and what are the real reasons which made it go through the circumstances it went through. We say that, first of all, the organizational base in north America is an organizational base with a dynamic characteristic.

This dynamics is at two levels: The first one is at the north America's level as the vast majority of the Muslim Brotherhood here are students. Therefore, we find them very prone to change, either for study reasons which is about two years for a brother and he changes his college, or, as far as residence is concerned, the Ikhwans change their address almost every semester, or, as far as moving outside of America, it is either a temporary departure and that usually happens during the summer vacation or the Christmas vacation, or a departure to work in the Orient for a limited time period, or it is a permanent departure which is when a brother ends his study or when an immigrants decides that it is time to return to his native country. The base changes about 70% almost every five years. Then, this dynamic nature had an impact on the course of work. Some of them were native effects. Some of these effects is that this prevents long-term planning due to the lack of the long-term stability of the base. Some of it is the difficulty of following up with the Ikhwans at the central level due to their constant changes of either their addresses or their residences. Some of that is, sometimes, the sudden disappearance of Ikhwans from the region or the city. Most likely this happens when the brother decides to terminate his studies and he packs his stuff and leaves without notifying those in charge in the first place.

Another negative effect is that this characteristic prevents supposed growth and makes the education of the individuals intermittent at times. As for the positive effects, they are: First, the exchange of ideas between the regions because when the Ikhwans move from one region to another they carry the experiences of this region to the other region. This was one of the positive things of the dynamics of the base. Also, the fact that it allowed new blood to be present as far as planning and execution are considered along the years. Also, the lack of formation of permanent isolated pockets because any organizational pocket might take some time..., a certain period of time and, after that, this pocket will disband either because the Ikhwans have departed the country or moved to other places. Therefore, an organizational pocket will not last.

And the other characteristic of this Movement is that the base has low density. By "low density" I mean that there is no large number of Ikhwans at one city. This, of course, has positive and negative effects. Among its negative effects on the Movement is the difficulty or forming educational or organizational levels. When a brother moves from one region or from one city to another, he might not find in the city he transferred to the educational level he was in. Also, the other negative effect is the difficulty of contacts and meetings. So, the method of contacts depended on was either the mail or the telephone. One of the flaws of that is that accountability and guidance are scarce. Among the positive effects for the..., for the..., the relative low density of the base is exerting the entire Ikhwan energy due to the lack of pressure and restrictions placed on the brother. Finding out a brother's genuineness, the working brother from the one who pretends to be a brother. When you place a brother in a position of responsibility in a...., in an atmosphere which has less accountability, the good nature or a good brother can produce even if there is no continuous direction or continuous accountability of his..., of his actions.

Also, there was another positive...., another positive which is training a brother on how to deal with non-brothers and planting the first seed for that. When a brother existed in a large Ikhwans gathering, his dealing will be with Ikhwans only. When a brother is alone or with a small Ikhwans' gathering, his dealing will be..., specially with non-Ikhwans, he will learn how to direct work through them. He will...., he will learn how to deal with them, the dealing..., dealing with a non-Ikhwan brother, as you know, is different from dealing with a brother. Also, there was a characteristic.., another characteristic for that Movement, which is the difference in tastes. Regardless of whether a brother is resident or temporary here, there are two kinds of Ikhwans who come to America: The first one found out about the call of the Ikhwans in north America and became regular in its ranks over here. Those brothers, even if they are residents, are the most Ikhwans who rush to defend and sacrifice for the sake of the Movement. Even if they are temporary, they will be, God's willing, new experiences and new blood in the movements of their countries.

As for the third kind, they originally came as Ikhwans and they became regular Ikhwans here. I mean, we call them "Imported Ikhwans" and those people are statues. Some of them came to study only. Therefore, working among the ranks of the Group comes in the second, the third or the fourth place for them. Some of them came to study but know that this life is for the Group so that he could reap its fruits in the afterlife, God's willing, and he places working in the ranks of the Group in the first place. Some of them came to study but see that working for the Group comes in two aspects: The first one, working among members of his homeland and after that comes general work in the ranks of the Group. Some of them came to study with a prior judg[e]ment about the Group over here regardless of it being right or wrong. Based on that, he makes a judg[e]ment and moves according to that. Some of them crone for work and they place their work first before the Group. Some of them came for work and know that this life is a farm for the afterlife and he sacrifices what he has for the sake of..., for the sake of this Dawa'a. These are the most important kinds of imported Ikhwans who come over here. Of course, every one of these kinds has its contribution, has its negative aspects and its positive aspects. Some of them were....., were a cause for the delay of hindering the work of the Group and its forward moving. Some of them were a cause for the Group to move forward. God's willing, everyone works with an intention for which we ask Almighty God to reward him for.

These are the three characteristics which describe the Ikhwan Movement in north America. In reality, it has unique characteristics. I mean, except in America and Europe, we do not find unified movements which work in that way, to be able to or try to melt all of the Ikhwans' experiences in a one pot, try to group all the Ikhwans under....er, under one umbrella. This experience had and still has many positive aspects for our Ikhwans, particularly Ikhwans of the Orient because it deepened the idea...., of the Group's unity. Here in America we find the practical application for this....., for this idea which is the Group's unity in one movement. Also, the positive and negative aspects of this work reflect here and we can achieve through them..., we can push these positive aspects forward and find solutions for these negative aspects and move through the negative aspects, God's willing, and turn them into positive aspects to benefit work. As for planning and the process of planning for the Group, it also went through historical phases. Some of them is the lack of clear plans neither for the Group or for general activism. I mean, the most important resolution the Group might have taken was who was going to be a member of the MSA 's executive committee. This was the most important resolution the Group could have taken during this phase.

Then, the first Ikhwans' plan was the five-year plan the Ikhwans put together lasting from '75-'80. Its primary focus was general work and dedication to the general work organizations. After that the five-year plan for '81-'85 and its focus was self-structure and settlement of the Dawa'a. All of these are plans are..., I mean, the one which put them together was the Shura Council. In the years '80 and '81, we started to work on a new kind of plans which is planning at the regions' level. Therefore, planning became..., planning became prominent at the regions' level as a system for work and as a system for accountability. As for this year, thanks be to God, the executive office has put together an annual work program on whose basis, God's willing, the region or the regions will build their plans for the current year. The plan of the executive office will be implemented beginning May '82 and, of course, ends in April '83.

When the executive office thought about putting this plan together, it really came in different stages such as gathering a group of Ikhwans who have experience and specialization in planning or management and they put together the first foundation or stone for this plan. It was then presented to the executive office after that and it compared it with the human potential in place and with the abilities of the Ikhwans in place and it chose from the bases which were put together by the first committee a group of goals which the executive office considered main goals which must be implemented during...., during this year, and it made a second group of goals secondary goals which it will try to implement this year if time permits and then hoped that these secondary goals will gradually move from the category of secondary goals to the main goals category and get their full share of implementation. After that, these main goals were divided..., some of which we will see in a little bit, because they had a general nature. They were divided into periodical goals which we will try to implement this year, God's willing.

The main goals which were approved by the executive office were five....., which were put together by the executive office and which were then approved by the Shura Council were, first of all: Strengthening the internal structure; second, administrative discipline; third, recruitment and settlement of the Dawa'a; four, energizing the organizations' work; five, energizing political work fronts. Also, it adopted eight of the secondary goals on top of which were: finance and investment; second, foreign relations; third, reviving women's activity; four, political awareness to members of the Group; five, securing the Group; six, special activity; seven, media; eight, taking advantage of human potentials. This is..., these arc the Group's main and the secondary goals for the next year of work, God's willing. Of course, along with these goals, we also had two things in front of us: The first thing is the reality of the Movement, and the second thing is what the Movement should be.

The reality of the Movement is that it is a students' Movement. What the Movement should be is to become a Movement for the residents because, Ikhwans, one of the things which we suffer from is that it is possible that all the Ikhwans in one city might leave it or that the fundamental people the Movement relies on in this city might collectively leave and, thus, leaving a sort of a vacuum behind them; a vacuum in work and also a vacuum in planning. That means that the five-year plans will not be effective in this region due to the absence of the Ikhwan element from it. Therefore, we had to take two simultaneous moves and with two harmonious wings: The first one is the reality or our attempt to implement the needs of the reality which is what the students' movement needs and that we also work hard to settle the Dawa'a. By "settlement of the Dawa'a", the Muslim Brotherhood Dawa'a is meant. It is not meant to spread Islam as spread of lslarn is a general thing and it is indeed a goal for each Muslim in general terms.

The second thing is the settlement of the Dawa'a and finding permanent fundamentals in the cities where Ikhwans now live in order to...er, in order for them to be the meeting points for the coming brothers. This way, work at any cities is not going to be disturbed due to the collective absence of a group of the Ikhwans. In reality, the issue of settling the Dawa'a in the past was not favored by a group of the Ikhwan who used to be here six or seven years ago, specially the students among them. They believed that the idea of settling the Dawa'a in north America is a waste of time and this, of course, was due to their students' view of work. Now, thanks be to God, we find that this phenomenon started to change. This change came in stages..., we can..., it came in forms which we can feel through the reality of general work. The first change was moving the Ikhwans from working at the branches of the MSA and the [Arab Youth Muslim] Association as branches whose activities are based on universities where they go a university to hold their activity, to what is called at that time "The Muslim House". The Muslim House was based on them purchasing a house near the university with Ikhwans living in a part of it and the rest of it becomes a mosque and it would also be a nucleus for the activity.

This was the first move the Ikhwans did. After that, the other move came where this Muslim House was not a goal by itself or it was no longer able to satisfy work as they started to move to somewhere else which are the Islamic centers. We notice that during the past two or three years that many of the students' gathering started to establish Islamic centers. This was also another healthy move for settling the Dawa'a as the presence of an Islamic center means the presence of residents, means the existence of contacts between students and the residents, means recruitment of the and winning them to the ranks of the Dawa'a, means forming permanent foundations in these cities. Then, what we have now or what we feel now is that there a bigger and bigger acceptance than the Ikhwans' base for this change and we ask God the Almighty to help us so that we can finish this mission which is the settlement of Dawa'a and that, by that, we would have permanent foundations in America which can benefit Islamic work generally speaking and may God reward you all good.

Um: If possible, let the brothers collect the questions from the audience... If possible, can you repeat to us the main goals and the secondary goals which were written by the Executive Office and which were approved by the Shura Council.

Ze: The main goals are five. They are: Strengthening the internal structure, administrative discipline, recruitment and settlement of the Dawa'a, energizing the organizations' work, energizing the political work fronts. As for the secondary goals, they are eight: first, financing and investment; second, foreign relations; third, reviving women's activity; four, political awareness to members of the Group; five, securing the Group; six, special activity; seven, media; eight, benefitting from human potentials.

Um: There is a question: What is the degree of connection between the Ikhwan. Group in America with the mother Group in Egypt?

[End of Side A]

Side B:

Ze: ... the dangers of these pockets are many; some of that is the fact that they hinder work, some of it is that they destabilize the ranks because the ranks then would he disconnected. Thanks be to God, we can currently say that there are no longer organizational pockets in the ranks of the Group. Thanks be to God, Lord of the Two Worlds, we were able to absorb these pockets during this past time. Organizational pockets most likely form due to a wrong idea adopted by some of the Ikhwans regarding means of work over here or they could be due to regional gatherings. So, they could come due to any of these forms.

Um: Er..., what is the relationship of the Islamic Group in Libya with the Ikhwan Group? Are they under the leadership of the Ikhwan Group or are they a separate group?

Ze: The Islamic Group...., the Islamic Group/Libya is a front..., a political action front. It is a political action front. Er..., who is the brother who asked the question? I just want to know if he means the Group which issues Al-Muslim magazine. Yes? Yes. So, my brother, it is a front..., it is a political front which was set up by the Libyan brothers in order to be able to move through it and issue Al-Muslim magazine. Yes, this front is overseen by brothers from the Ikhwans. They are, I mean, they're from Libya and their native country was Libya. They are associated with the Group and they're affiliated with the Group. And the Group directs the path of this group and this..., or this front through the presence of the adherent Libyan brothers in the Movement and who work in this front.

Um: Don't you see that the Movement's methods and programs in America should be different from the methods and programs in the Arab countries or from the Arab countries due to the change of the place and the available sources, the type of individuals and the maxim benefit from the means available in America? For instance, the cultural programs are very weak. Recruitment methods are limited and are being restricted.

Ze: By God, my brother, we really see that..., that the methods..., we really see that our methods and means are different from the Orient. We did not take or borrow a method or a means from the Orient unless it was compatible with the reality of the Islamic Movement over here. Our methods are always driven from the nature of the organizational base..., from the nature of the...er, from the nature of the country which is America and also from the nature of the base from which we move, the people we move between are mostly highly-educated youth. They are college youth and they are also youth who are aware. They are more aware than the youth who are of the same stage or age in the Orient. The reason..., the reason of this awareness and maturity is their presence in America, not because they are in America, I mean, America has nothing to do with it but, because of their presence in America, they have no mother to wash their clothes or a father who gives them their allowance at the end of the month. They have to depend on themselves in balancing his household budget, for instance, purchase their own stuff, cook for themselves if they are single, to wash their clothes if they are single, all of these things. Also, they have to deal and interact with society directly. All of that, Ikhwans, without....er, I mean, without family protection. I mean the family is not..., without the family cover or armor which used to protect him in his country. All of these will bring about more awareness and maturity.

This is the base which we move through. Therefore, our recruitment methods are different. Er..., in reality, I don't know why the brother says that...er, that our recruitment is weak while we are considered...., even considered in the view of many of the Orient's movements to be an open movement and that we are a movement which is lax in conditions despite the fact that we don't think that we are lax in the conditions but, this is their view...., their view of us.

Er...., we are experiencing a surge in recruitment. Let me take advantage of this opportunity and tell you what are..., or how the individuals are recruited so that the Ikhwans are up to speed. During one of its meeting, an Usra nominates a group of the Ikhwans or a group of Muslim youth who are present to become regular in the work or to become regular at the ranks of the Group. Through the Naquib, an Usra submits these names to the Masul of the region or the Masul of the district. After that, the Masul of the region contacts ... , he takes these names and contacts the coordinators of these countries..., of that country. Meaning that a brother who is coming from Jordan, we would contact the Jordan's coordinators. We inquire about him and see if there is any objection to bringing him on board. After that, he is to wait two weeks. If the coordinator does not rely during this time period, then the matter is discussed during the meeting of the region's council. I mean, the matter is up to the region itself as they are the ones who will decide. After that, a region is to decide if the brother is to become regular...., this brother to become regular at the Group's ranks or not according to the reasons and according to what it sees. I believe that, this way, we bypassed a lot of the central issues and bypassed many of the steps which were in place at some point in order to speed up the assimilation of the Ikhwans.

What an Usra should do before that is...., there are...., our methods are clear and known as there is an individual contact and after that come the open Usras or the open Halaqas and then, when the brother has completed the open Halaqas, he can then become regular...., if the Usra sees that, he can become regular at the General Movement. That if he is a new brother. Of course, if he is a regular brother in his country, of course, he would be coming with a letter or recommendation through the coordinator. He can become regular maybe in a period of three months at the most, he would become regular at the Usras. Yes, some special cases might happen whereby the Ikhwans are late for a reason or another. But, generally speaking, the matter does not take more than three months and the brother who just came or the imported brother will become regular, he will become regular at the Movement. Er..., of course, we said that because the base from which we move is a mature base, we might at times jump through some of these circles. We might, for instance, jump through the open Usra and the Group is asked to make a brother regular right after the individual contact, for instance. Of course, a region then has the right to consider this..., to consider such jumps and whether they are proper or not.

As for the educational programs, in reality the program which is in your hands...., this program is the first section...., this is a program for the open Usras. And the second section is the beginners' program. We are still putting programs together and the Education Office, may God reward them all good, are now working on the Workers' programs and the Naquibs' programs. God's willing, they will be in your hands during the summer's months if God makes it easy. Then..., yes, an imported brother in particular, the one who has been in the Dawa'a for long, might find these programs are below...., below his level because he might have taken them ten years ago. But, we tell him, "Brother, just to be reminded. It is good to be reminded. These are very good things to re-examine because they are fundamentals of the Dawa'a during this time period". God's willing, the moment the Workers' and the Naquibs' programs arrive, this crisis will be resolved.

Um: There is a group of questions almost all of which are about one subject which is a remark that some of the movements have not joined the Movement here in America such as the Saudis, just to cite one o f their examples. So,... I mean.

Ze: In reality, it is the only movement, the Saudis. They have not joined. Only the imported brothers among them are not regulars. I mean, it means that there is a home product. I reality, our work among the Saudis is good in the areas where they congregate such as..., such as southern California and such as...., different regions where they congregate. Our work among them is good. As for the Saudi brothers who came originally as Ikhwans, they had a different point of view whereby they did not want to become regular at the Movement here. We do not agree with them on that but we also respect the decision they made and we ask Almighty God that we meet at the end. If we..., if all of us work to please Almighty God first and foremost, we will meet. And, if anyone among us is working for something within him or out of desire, we will not meet. We ask Almighty God to make both of us to work to please God and, God's willing, we will meet soon in a unified Movement.

Um: What is your opinion regarding the formation of one or multiple fronts for the Group without having the base which represents the Ikhwans, meaning distributing the efforts of the brothers who are the Group without a base in order to stay ahead of the events.

Ze: By God, fronts are one method...., one method for grouping and are one method to communicate the Ikhwan's thought. They are one method to communicate the Ikhwan's point of view. A front is not formed until after a study and after an exhaustive study. I mean, the last front formed by the Group is the Islamic Association for Palestine. So, Ikhwans, this did not come out over night or it was not like the Ikhwans who are in charge went to sleep, dreamed about it and met the next day and decided to do it. Not at all, by God. This went through lengthy meetings and took long discussions. Many specialized auxiliary committees were formed which were examining this work, they were examining this work from different angles, from the angle of the benefit of such work, from the angle of, for instance, the human resources we have, from an angle of how this front would benefit us in communicating the brothers' point of view. Then, generally speaking, we don't work out of vacuum if that is what is meant. As for distributing the brothers' efforts, yes, in some of the regions where few Ikhwans exist, there will really be a heavy pressure on them because, in addition to that, they have to be members of the *MSA*, The [Muslim Arab Youth] Association and, if they're Palestinians for instance, they will have to be members in the Islamic Association for Palestine. Yes, it is correct, this would place additional burdens or weight on the brother. But, an active and a smart brother can benefit from the efforts of the Islamists who are around him, for instance. He can distribute some of these burdens in a way which does not let planning get out of the hands of the Group in the region. He can benefit from the resources around him because *we*, Ikhwans, cannot work with our resources alone and our number is limited.

So, let every brother check the percentage of the Ikhwans against the number of existing Muslims and not the entire Muslims. But, let's say, the adherent Muslims who attend the Friday prayers, for instance. If you check the percentage, you won't find the Ikhwans percentage in people more than 1% which is a tiny percentage, of course. It is possible, of course, that you think that this 1% can not carry the entire work burden. But, if you manage to direct the resources which arc available to it and when you can benefit from it, this burden will then become less.

Um: In order to settle the Dawa'a, is there planning by you by asking that the brothers who have experience to remain here?

Ze: My brother, one of the stage goals which were set regarding the settlement of the Dawa'a is encouraging the brothers who cannot return to their countries ... , they cannot return to their countries for either political, economic or whatever reasons to settle here in America. We encourage this phenomenon in this stage, that the Ikhwans who cannot return to their countries we encourage them to stay. We can provide him with all the available means or advice on how to remain in this..., in this country and to work as one of the goals of settling the Dawa'a or, excuse me, as one of the methods of settling the Dawa'a.

Um: By "Securing the Group", do you mean military securing? And, if it is that, would you explain to us a little bit the means to achieve it.

Ze: No. Mili[t]ary work is listed under "Special work". "Special work" means military work. "Securing the Group" is the Groups' security, the Group's security against outside dangers. For instance, to monitor the suspicious movements on the...., which exist on the American front such as Zionism, Masonry....etc. Monitoring the suspicious movements or the sides, the government bodies such as the *CIA, FBI...etc,* so that we find out if they are monitoring us, are we not being monitored, how can we get rid of them. That's what is meant by "Securing the Group".

Um: There is a question which we will ask..., I mean, we will ask them individually as none of them relate to the other. The resources and freedoms which are available in north America are bigger than what is available in the Islamic world. Despite that, organizational work methods have not changed.

Ze: By God, I believe that the methods are different. If the asking brother is from Iraq, he would know that it is impossible to have such a gathering in Iraq and this is one of the methods. If the asking brother is from Jordan, for instance, he would know that it is not possible to have military training in Jordan, for instance, while here in America, there is weapons training in many of the Ikhwans' camps. Er...., if the brother is from Libya, he would know that the Islamic Movement has not been able to form due to the pressure which is on the..., on the people, but it succeeded in growing in America. Our methods, Ikhwans, then are different then even though we might use the same concepts. I mean, we resort to secrecy but the secrecy at our end might take a position that is different from what is in the Orient, for instance. Secrecy over there might be absolute. It might be absolute even among the ranks of the Group. For instance, until now, most of the movements do not know who is the General Masul of the movement when he is among their ranks and neither do they know who are members of the executive office or who is the Masul of the Organization Office, who is the Masul of the Financial Office and so forth. Over here, the brothers know who are the Group's General Masul. Most of the Ikhwans know who is the Masul of the Organization Office. Most of the Naquibs know who are the members of the Executive Office and so on. This means that there is a change in the means. And so on, we can now..., speak about the fronts, for instance. *For* instance, the brothers in Egypt don't have fronts in the same broad way we have in America and the fronts are one of the means and so on. Then, Ikhwans, our means are really different. They might carry the same name but the content is different.

Um: There is a two-fold question: Why there was a difference in...., or why did the Ikhwans disagree during their conferences in the 60's and also, why are women allowed to attend the conferences?

Ze: Of course, during that time, this is regarding why were the wives of the Ikhwans in the 60's or even the beginning of the 70's to attend the Ikhwans' conferences? This is the input of the leadership. I mean, I don't want to say why and neither do I want to speak on their behalf. This was the input of the leadership then. And I really believe that this input was proper. I mean, Had I been at the same time in the same situation, I would have given the same input because the issue was an a issue of grouping, the issue was an issue of grouping. And the social aspect of the grouping issue is very important. We now ask why does this happen in the present time? Yes, during our conferences, the adherent Sisters attend. And we have awing called The Muslim Sisters and we have a Masul for them in the Executive Office. My brothers, work cannot be done...., the Ikhwans work cannot be successful unless the women's part of it goes side by side. My brother, if you are married and your wife is not among of the Sisters, you should be the first one to understand this point. You would feel that there is a deficiency, there is a restriction on your work and your moving. Just because she is a Sister mean she will be informed of every big and small issue in the Movement? No. Because she is a Sister she can understand your feeling, she can make available to you the atmosphere for work. But, if she is not a Sister, you can try to come to the camp and [she is like], "How is it that you're going to leave me and go over there" ....etc. And she starts asking you, "How about the boy? What if he gets sick and how is going to come to take him to the doctor" and get you many excuses. Why? Because she does not understand the nature of your work and the nature of your movement. But, if she is a Sister, if she..., and by God we have found these examples among the Sisters, that she had just gave birth, just delivered two or three days ago and her husband leaves her and attend Ikhwan camps. If he tells her, "I will stay to take care of you", she would tell him, "No". She does not accept.

There is a difference, Ikhwans, between a brother who finds this atmosphere at work and a brother who finds the other atmosphere. As for the reasons for the problems which happened in the Ikhwans camps, it was because for the inclination far change or moving from a gathering to a formation and a selection, from a gathering of Islamists, kind people and stuff, Ok, let it be good and Ok, let's go, let's go, let's go, come over and let's get together, from a lake-all movement to a precise and a movement. This, Ikhwans, are the reasons which made the conferences of the end of the 70's have a special characteristic, the ones which always ended with tears and pain. But, thanks be to Almighty God, their outcome....er, their outcome is this camp and those Ikhwans.

Um: One of the brothers is asking about what is meant with the Executive Office. But, I just wanted to explain to the brother that brother Munzir is not...., is not the director of the Executive Office as he mentioned but he is the Masul of the Organization Office.

Ze: My brother, the Executive Office is the Group's Executive Leadership. The Executive Office is divided into offices. Through these offices, the affairs of the Group are run. Among them is the Organization Office..., the Organization Office which oversees the...er, over the regions and the Usras of the Group. And among them is the Education Office which oversees the preparation of cultural programs for the Ikhwans or the educational [programs] for the Ikhwans and also prepares the training programs for the Ikhwans in the different fields and various specializations among which is the Political Office which submits political analysis to the Ikhwans and also the Sisters Office which runs and promotes the activity of the Sisters Division, Among them is, of course, the Secretariat General which is the Movement's Secretary. These are the executive offices which ace available now. They are the Group's Executive Leadership.

Ok, as for the Organizational Skeleton....er, the Group's Organizational Skeleton begins first of all from the highest..., it is the highest..., the highest organization in the Group is the Organizational Conference. The Organizational Conference is a conference...., is a stemming from the Ikhwans bases; every Usra elects one or two according to its number. This brother represents the Usra in the Organizational Conference which is the highest body in the Ikhwan. After that, the Shura Council comes then the Executive Office. The Shura Council...., what did the brother ask....? Er...., this is how it is.

The Shura Council, of course, has many duties among which are....,just let me see the...., it is better that I read them from the by-laws which is better than reciting them from memory. Yes. Duties...., Duties and responsibilities of the Shura Council: It has the duties of planning, charting the general policies and the programs which achieve the goals of the Group which are specified in the course, its resolutions are binding to the Group and only the General Organizational Conference can modify them or annul them which has the right to modify or annul resolutions of the Executive Office. It follows up on the implementation of the Group's policies and programs, it directs them and it directs the Executive Office and it forms dedicated committees...., branching committees to assist in that. It oversees that and directs them in what ensures the implementation of the policies. It elects the Group's General Masul and the Executive Office and it has..., it has the right to guide, hold accountable and...[UI] and the General Masul is to be elected among the elected members of the Council only. These are the duties of the Executive Office....er, the Shura Council.

As for the duties of the Executive Office, it executes and follows up on the works of the Group and its different bodies according to the general policy and the resolutions...., and the resolutions issued by the Shura Council. It has to follow up and guide the activities of the general work organization and to make sure they run according to the Group's plan with what achieves its goals. It submits a periodical report to the Shura Council about its work and the activity of...., the activity of the domestic bodies and the general organizations. The Office distributes its duties to its members according to the internal bylaws. The Sisters are to have a special office which is affiliated with the Group's bodies and a special bylaws approved by the Shura Council determine the method of its formation and its responsibilities. It then talks about the quorum and it talks about the office's term which ends with the end of the Shura Council's term. This the.... As for the specialized office, I believe it will take long if we wanted to explain the duty of each office.

Um: You mentioned that there is a weapons training at the Ikhwans' camps but I did not see that at all in the mid-southern region camps. So, would you explain to us the reasons.

Ze: By God, the first thing is that you thank God and praise him because you found a camp to meet in. You know that, for instance, Oklahoma has become a blocked area for you. You cannot meet in it in the first place, right? Then, the nature.... What'! [Unintelligible talk from the audience] Yes, I'm sorry. I thought..., Ok. My brothers, according to what we learned..., to what I learned in Oklahoma they started to be strict about letting Muslims use the camps. They would ask them, for instance, to submit their name and they would ask you to bring an ID or something to prove your name. I learned that they were going on a *picnic* recently, a trip, and the police came asking each person to give..., to present a,...er, to show his ID or even his *visa.* These harassments exist then in the state of Oklahoma, for instance. And these are among the reasons which made our brothers in the reason to have their camp here in Missouri. Right, my brother? Then, the circumstances which a region goes through are the ones which determine. In some of the regions when they go to a camp, they take two things, they would request a camp which has a *range,* a shooting *range* and one which has a range to shoot, one which has a range which they use for shooting. You would find that in some of the camps. They would get an advance permit for that. I mean, I don't know the possibility of having these camps here and also whether the pressure which exists in Oklahoma...., and whether they will have a weapons training in the other regions...., these harassments might continue, I mean, become contagious to the other regions.

Um: Do you see that the latest events in Syria had an impact on the Group's policy in America and in particularly the political aspect. Between brackets, "To explain, showing flexibility in dealing with non-Muslim movements".

Ze: Yes, there is no doubt that the Group here in America was impacted at all of its levels with Syria events. And...., work, Ikhwans...., I mean, what is happening in...., or what happened in Syria...., Syria has become one of the priorities of Ikhwans' political activism in north America. I will speak about that in details I believe in a lecture immediately following this one which will be about the Ikhwans of Syria and I believe that I will give the opportunity to the lecturing brother to reply to these questions. The asking brother should ask the other lecturing brother should he not find in the previous lecture what satisfies him or what replies to this question, God's willing.

Um Er..., there is a brother who is inquiring about the lack of brothers from Tunisia, Algeria and Morocco and even Yemen and a brother who is asking about..., I mean, he wants information about the Ikhwans in Canada.

Ze: The lack of Algerian or Tunisian Ikhwans is because their presence in America is scarce. My brothers, you know that Algeria and Tunisia have a French culture, the countries have a French culture. Therefore, most of its citizens prefer to go to France rather than come to America. In addition to the fact that the Islamic movement over there in the two countries is a budding movement. They're still new. Despite of that, it has been dealt a blow which it did not recover from yet. It did not talk even though it was hit savagely and, of course, you know what happened in Tunisia. This is one of the reasons which makes the presence of the Tunisian brothers scarce among us. Of course, this does not mean that you should not work among good Tunisian congregation. You should work among them, form Usras, you should initiate individual contacts with them....etc. As for Yemen, Ikhwans, it is a poor country. Yemen is a poor country. It cannot send exchange students to America and it cannot...., I mean, as a government...., and, as individuals, they cannot send their sons at their expense. I mean, if you have $100 over there, you can live an entire year with it. You would live comfortably and you might be considered among the rich. Not among the rich but, I mean, the comfortable ones.

Therefore, all of that makes the percentage of educated Yemenis small. This does not mean there is not a large Yemeni community. There is a very large Yemeni labor community in America. It is centered in two spots: the first one is what they call the San Joacquim

Valley. It is an agricultural area in California and the other place is Detroit in the automobile factories. If there to take the Yemeni workers out o f Detroit, the automobile industry would stop. According to what I found out from the Masul of the region Detroit is under, thanks be to God, we were able for the time to recruit three Yemeni workers and, God's willing, they will be a pillar for us to enter into that gathering.

Um: There are four remaining questions but it seems that time is up even though we would have liked for you to answer all of them. Er..., we ask Almighty God to benefit us with what we heard and to increase our knowledge. May God reward you well. God's peace, mercy and blessings to you.

Ze: Ikhwans, you posed questions and I now have questions. I would like to know -through raising of hands- about your receiving of the Group's periodicals. First of all, I will start with al-Bayan [The Declaration] periodical. It is a magazine which is published bi-monthly. How many brother saw the 4th issue? Let him raise his hand. Al-Bayan's 4th issue. There is hesitation. Ok. As far as the periodicals of the Education Office, the Darb al-Dowat [Path o f the Callers], how many brothers saw it? Ok. Regarding the political statement sent by the Group about the Syria events and about the national coalition, how many brother received it? Read it, of course, and saw it. By God.... My brother, why are you.... Where are you, my brother, may God keep you?

Um: From Colorado.

Ze: Yes. You did not receive the statement? Who is your Naquib? Or are you the Naquib?

Um: .... [UI].

Ze: Ok, our brothers, I would like to announce two things: Our periodicals, the periodicals which the Group sends in a regular way are two: The first one is al-Bayan bulletin and the second one is Darb al-Dowat. So, I hope that the Ikhwans ask their Naquibs every now and then about these periodicals whether they received them. Also, I ask the Naquibs to ask the Masul of the region every now and then whether if they received these periodicals because we don't this effort to be put and then they don't reach the bases which are supposed to be the ones who benefit from them. May God reward yo[u] well.

Unidentified noise for few seconds before recording stops.

References

[1] FBI Search Warrant "A Pallet of Documents in the Driveway of 4502 Whistler Court, Annandale, Virginia," August 23, 2004, accessed at: http://www.investigativeproject.org/documents/case_docs/1524.pdf

[2] "An Explanatory Memorandum on the General Strategic Goals for the Group In North America," Center for Security Policy Press, 2013. Also available at the North Texas District Court Website, as Elbarasse Search-3, at http://coop.txnd.uscourts.gov/judges/hlf2/09-25-08/Elbarasse%20Search%203.pdf

[3] For an example of this effort, see Patrick Poole, "Pulitzer Prize Winner Hawks 'Protocols of the Elders of the Anti-Islam Movement' in the New Yorker," PJ Media, May 13, 2015, https://pjmedia.com/tatler/2015/05/13/pulitzer-prize-winners-journalistic-malpractice-over-the-u-s-muslim-brotherhood/ and Kyle Shideler, "Mohammed Akram and the Explanatory Memorandum Still Matter," Center for Security Policy, May 18, 2015, http://www.centerforsecuritypolicy.org/2015/05/18/mohammad-akram-and-explanatory-memo-still-matter/

[4] Al-Noman is also identified (under the transliteration Zaid Naman) as a member of the U.S. Muslim Brotherhood Executive Office, in the 1992 Phone Directory also submitted at the Holy Land Foundation trial. See: http://www.investigativeproject.org/documents/case_docs/1083.pdf

[5] "Elbarasse Search-2," page 7, http://coop.txnd.uscourts.gov/judges/hlf2/09-25-08/Elbarasse%20Search%202.pdf

[6] The 1987 "long term plan" is also referenced in the October 25, 1991, document entitled "Shura Council Report on the Future of the Group Workpaper #l," also found during the Elbarasse search and entered into evidence at the Holy Land Foundation Trial as "Elbarasse Search-1," which gives a "Historical Outlook" of the U.S. MB that largely substantiates the statements made by Al-Noman. http://coop.txnd.uscourts.gov/judges/hlf2/09-25-08/Elbarasse%20Search%201.pdf

[7] Noreen S. Ahmed-Ullah, Sam Roe and Laurie Cohen, "A Rare Look at Secretive Brotherhood in America," *Chicago Tribune*, September 19, 2004, http://www.chicagotribune.com/news/watchdog/chi-0409190261sep19-story.html#page=3 The Chicago Tribune article gives the date as 1963, but "El-

barasse Search-1" cites the year 1962, and so we will utilize the date given by the Brothers themselves.

[8] "Elbarasse Search-2," page 7, http://coop.txnd.uscourts.gov/judges/hlf2/09-25-08/Elbarasse%20Search%202.pdf

[9] Hisham AlTalib, "Training Guide for Islamic Workers," International Institute of Islamic Thought, 1991, pg. 6.

[10] Kyle Shideler and David Daoud, "The International Institute of Islamic Thought: The Muslim Brotherhood's Think Tank," July 28, 2014, Center for Security Policy Press, http://www.centerforsecuritypolicy.org/wp-content/uploads/2014/07/IIIT-Backgrounder-final-07-28-14-1.pdf. See also: Michelle Malkin, "Who Is White House visitor Hisham Altalib?" MichelleMalkin.com, October 22, 2012, http://michellemalkin.com/2012/10/22/reminder-who-is-white-house-visitor-hisham-al-talib/22 . Al Taqwa Bank was delisted as a Specially Designated entity in February 2015, https://www.treasury.gov/resource-center/sanctions/OFAC-Enforcement/Pages/20150226.aspx

[11] "Elbarasse Search-1," http://coop.txnd.uscourts.gov/judges/hlf2/09-25-08/Elbarasse%20Search%201.pdf

[12] Shamim A. Siddiqui, "Methodology of Dawah," Forum for Islamic Work, 1989. For more on Siddiqui and his role, see: Stephen Coughlin, "Catastrophic Failure: Blindfolding America in the Face of Jihad," Center for Security Policy Press, 2015, pg. 190.

[13] See the work of Shafi'i Islamic law, *Reliance of the Traveller*, approved by Muslim Brotherhood-linked groups the Fiqh Council of North America and the International Institute of Islamic Thought. *Reliance* notes Dawa as a precondition to Jihad, in Book 0 Justice, o.9.8.

[14] Sayyid Qutb, "Milestones: Special Edition," Ed. A.B. Mehri, Maktabah Booksellers and Publishers, Birmingham, 2006.

[15] "An Explanatory Memorandum on the General Strategic Goals for the Group In North America," Center for Security Policy Press, 2013. Also available at the North Texas District Court Website, as Elbarasse Search-3, at http://coop.txnd.uscourts.gov/judges/hlf2/09-25-08/Elbarasse%20Search%203.pdf

16 https://petitions.whitehouse.gov/response/response-we-people-petition-muslim-brotherhood

17 Mitchell, Richard P. The Society of the Muslim Brothers, London: Oxford UP, 1969. Pg. 30-32.

18 Ibid. Pg. 56.

19 "Elbarasse Search-3," http://coop.txnd.uscourts.gov/judges/hlf2/09-25-08/Elbarasse%20Search%203.pdf

20 Reuters, "Ex-Florida University Professor Deported over ties to Palestinian Islamic Jihad," February 7, 2015, http://www.jpost.com/International/Ex-Florida-University-professor-deported-over-ties-to-Palestinian-Islamic-Jihad-390265

21 Steven Emerson, "New Disclosures Tighten ISNA-Muslim Brotherhood Bonds," July 22, 2008, http://www.investigativeproject.org/730/new-disclosures-tighten-isna-muslim-brotherhood-bonds

22 David Kane, "Affidavit in Support of Application for Search Warrant (October 2003: In the Matter of Searches of 555 Grove Street and Herndon, VA and Related Locations" U.S. District Court (Eastern District of VA), available at: https://www.investigativeproject.org/documents/case_docs/891.pdf

23 "Charter of The Center for Studies Intelligence and Information," June 1981, http://www.investigativeproject.org/documents/case_docs/533.pdf

24 "Brief of the United States," No. 09-10560 IN THE UNITED STATES COURT OF APPEALS FOR THE FIFTH CIRCUIT UNITED STATES OF AMERICA, Plaintiff-Appellee, v. HOLY LAND FOUNDATION FOR RELIEF AND DEVELOPMENT, et. al., Appellants, http://www.investigativeproject.org/documents/case_docs/1474.pdf

25 "Marzook Payments to IAP," http://coop.txnd.uscourts.gov/judges/hlf2/09-29-08/Marzook%20IAP.pdf

26 "Philly Meeting Summary," http://coop.txnd.uscourts.gov/judges/hlf2/09-29-08/Philly%20Meeting%20Summary.pdf

27 "Elbarasse Search-19," http://coop.txnd.uscourts.gov/judges/hlf2/09-29-08/Elbarasse%20Search%2019.pdf